See the USA

NASHVILLE
TENNESSEE

by
Paul J. Deegan

CRESTWOOD HOUSE
New York

LIBRARY OF CONGRESS CATALOGING IN PUBLICATION DATA

Deegan, Paul J.
  Nashville, Tennessee / by Paul J. Deegan : edited by Marion Dane Bauer

  p. cm. — (See the U.S.A.)
  Includes index.
  SUMMARY: Highlights the attractions of Nashville, Tennessee, and the surrounding area, with an emphasis on Opryland and the other landmarks associated with the country music industry.
  1. Nashville (Tenn.)—Description—Juvenile literature. 2. Nashville Region (Tenn.)—Description and travel—Juvenile literature. 3. Country music—Tennessee—Nashville—Juvenile literature. 4. Musical landmarks—Tennessee—Nashville—Juvenile literature. [1. Nashville (Tenn.)—Description—Guides. 2. Musical landmarks—Tennessee—Nashville.] I. Bauer, Marion Dane. II. Title. III. Series.
  F444.N24D43   1989   976.8'55—dc20   89-32913
  ISBN 0-89686-468-5   CIP
                                                                                    AC

PHOTO CREDITS

Cover: Nashville Area Chamber of Commerce
Nashville Area Chamber of Commerce: 4, 12, 14, 17, 18, 28, 32, 33, 35, 37, 38, 42-43
Journalism Services: (H. Rick Bamman) 6, 25, 26, 31; (Richard Day) 7
Third Coast Stock Source: 8; (Todd S. Dacquisto) 10; (Alan R. Bagg) 13, 15, 19, 40; (Todd V. Phillips) 20, 21, 22

Opryland USA, Grand Ole Opry, General Jackson, The Nashville Network, Opryland, Opryland Hotel, and all related marks owned by Opryland USA, Inc are utilized in this publication with the specific approval of Opryland USA, Inc.

Edited by Marion Dane Bauer

CRESTWOOD HOUSE

Macmillan Publishing Company
866 Third Avenue
New York, NY 10022
Collier Macmillan Canada, Inc.

Produced by Carnival Enterprises

Printed in the United States of America

First Edition

10 9 8 7 6 5 4 3 2 1

CONTENTS

Nashville: Music City, U.S.A.

What comes to mind when you think of Nashville, Tennessee? The answer for most people is music. Nashville especially brings to mind country music, which is based on the folk music of rural America. Country music has especially strong roots in the southern and southwestern states.

Nashville is the self-styled "Music City, U.S.A." It is a major center for recording and publishing music. So many songs are recorded and published here that Nashville rivals much bigger cities like New York and Los Angeles.

Nashville became Music City, U.S.A., because of a famous radio show. The **Grand Ole Opry** began over 60 years ago. The show soon drew musicians and singers to Nashville. Eventually a large industry developed around these performers. Some people now call Nashville the premier recording center in North America.

The city is now known throughout the world for its country music stars. There is even something called the "Nashville Sound." But bluegrass and blues music thrive here as well. You can also hear Broadway show tunes.

This reputation for music has made Nashville famous. When you go to Nashville, you won't be the only visitor there. Tourism is a multi-million-dollar business in Nashville. Sixteen airlines serve this medium-sized city.

Nashville has other prominent industries, too. It is a city of banks and insurance companies. These have given Nashville another nickname, the "Wall Street of the South." The city is also a manufacturing center, with about 700 industries. Some religious denominations are headquartered here, and so are several religious publishing houses.

Nashville also is known as the "Athens of the South." This is

Many country music stars, including Randy Travis, can be seen in and around Nashville, Tennessee. Nashville is a major center for recording and publishing music.

Nashville is in the center of Tennessee. It has a population of 510,000.

because 16 colleges and universities are located here. There are two teaching hospitals as well.

Nashville has sometimes been called the "City of Parks." Its park system has been cited as among the best in the nation. Nashville's 65 parks cover some 6,500 acres. Six large lakes are within easy driving distance of the city.

A River City

Nashville has a population of about 510,000. It is located on the **Cumberland River** and is near the center of Tennessee. Nashville is nestled in rolling hills. Three interstate highways, 24, 40, and 65, meet in the city.

Nashville has generally warm weather. Even in the coldest months, the temperature doesn't fall much below 40 degrees.

Nashville is within 200 miles of several large cities. **Memphis, Tennessee,** is to the southwest. The Tennessee cities of **Chattanooga** and **Knoxville** are to the southeast and east. **Louisville, Kentucky,** is to the north. **Birmingham, Alabama,** is south of Nashville.

Tourists enjoy coming to Nashville because it has a moderate climate. Daytime temperatures are in the mid 60s by the end of March. Summers are very warm and humid. Tourists are attracted by the changing of the leaves in autumn. In central Tennessee, the days remain warm until November. The weather is cooler from November through March. However, the average daily high in January, the coldest month, is still 46 degrees. There is snowfall, usually in January and February.

A tourist information center is located just off Interstate 65 at the James Robertson Parkway. This center is operated by the Convention and Visitors Division of the Nashville Area Chamber of Commerce. It is just northeast of downtown Nashville. It is open seven days a week.

Overview of Things to Do

Nashville's Chamber of Commerce slogan is "Let Us Entertain You." And that the city can do. Some seven million visitors accept the invitation each year—and there are many things for kids to do.

A must stop for you in Nashville has to be **Opryland USA** and the many exciting rides in its amusement park, **Opryland**. There also may be an opportunity to see a television show being taped.

Another major attraction is **Music Row.** Here you may want to

Many visitors to Opryland enjoy the rides just as much as the music.

record a "hit song" at **Recording Studios of America.** You will also find several music museums here.

Two of Nashville's museums will hold your attention for hours. They are the **Cumberland Science Museum** and the **Tennessee State Museum.**

Adults and children will enjoy the **Nashville Toy Museum** on Music Valley Drive. It has a collection of toy soldiers from around the world. Teddy bears, dolls, and train sets are also displayed.

If you visit Nashville in the summer, you will want to visit **Wave Country,** one of the largest wave-action pools in the south. It is located on Two Rivers Parkway and is open between Memorial Day and Labor Day.

What kid wouldn't want to ride an old-fashioned trolley? Trolleys run in downtown Nashville. And horse-drawn carriages have recently become another part of the downtown Nashville scene.

A Fort Becomes a City

Two pioneers from North Carolina founded Nashville in the winter of 1779–1780. They chose the site for several reasons. It had a plentiful supply of water. There were fertile farmlands and forests. And there were salt springs, which is why the area was first called French Salt Lick or Big Salt Lick. Shawnee Native Americans once lived in the area.

The first settlers built forts on both sides of the Cumberland River. One was named **Fort Nashborough** after **Francis Nash,** a Revolutionary War general. The river town took his name—Nashville—in 1784.

Tennessee became a state in 1796. Ten years later, Nashville was chartered as a city. From 1812 to 1815 it was the capital of Tennessee. It became the permanent capital in 1843.

Nashville was one of the headquarters of the Confederacy during the Civil War. Then the city came under control of Union

There are many places to hear live music in Nashville.

troops in 1862. Two years later, it was the site of one of the final major battles of the Civil War. Confederate forces under **General John Bell Hood** moved to recapture the city in December 1864. The Union army destroyed almost the entire Confederate force. The victory secured all of Tennessee for the Union.

Opryland USA

In the late 1960s, some people from the Grand Ole Opry decided to build a theme park in Nashville. They knew what they wanted for a theme: music — and lots of it.

They followed through on their idea, and today you can visit one of the nation's most popular attractions. Opryland is a park nicknamed "The Home of American Music." Its operators say it is "unique in the park industry."

Opryland provides much for kids to see and do. Opryland says it "offers more than any guest can absorb in a single day."

Opryland is one of many businesses. Opryland USA is an umbrella term describing them all. Included are entertainment, broadcasting, and hospitality businesses.

Among the businesses owned by Opryland USA are Opryland (the theme park), the **General Jackson Showboat, The Nashville Network (TNN),** and the **Opryland Hotel.** There are also a television syndication business, a songwriting and music publishing business, and a recording business.

Opryland USA is nine miles northwest of downtown Nashville. This is about a 15-minute drive. Opryland USA is just west of Briley Parkway. The Cumberland River is on the west side of the complex.

Opryland USA occupies 406 acres of wooded, rolling hills. The parking area for Opryland, Grand Ole Opry, and the *General Jackson* is at the south end of Opryland USA. The parking area is marked with its own exit from Briley Parkway.

A Musical Entertainment Theme Park

Your visit to Opryland, the musical theme park, no doubt will be a highlight of your trip to Nashville. It covers 120 acres and offers 21 rides and adventures. And don't forget the park's live musical productions.

The park is divided into several areas. They have such names as the New Orleans area, the Hill Country area, Do Wah Diddy City, and the State Fair area.

One ride you probably won't want to miss is the Grizzly River Rampage. This is the park's own white-water rafting river. It is located in the ten-acre Grizzly Country area. You will get wet as you free-float down the river. The ride takes you on a 12-passenger raft through rapids, past boulders, and through a cave. The

Opryland's Wabash Cannonball takes visitors on a hair-raising, 50-mile-an-hour ride.

river was designed to imitate a raging river in the Great Smoky Mountains, which are in eastern Tennessee.

The Wabash Cannonball will turn you upside down. It is a corkscrew roller coaster. It speeds over a 1,200-foot track at 50 miles per hour. The track includes two giant loops.

If you want a slower pace, there is the Sky Ride. Swiss cable cars travel over 1,100 feet. The cars are four-passenger cabins. The ride offers a great view of Opryland and the **Grand Ole Opry House.**

For smaller kids, an entire area is devoted to kiddie rides. These include the Red Baron Airplanes, the Mini Rock 'n' Roller Coaster, and the Mini Ferris Wheel.

The Big "G" Kid Stuff is an activity area for even younger chil-

For a relaxed tour of Opryland, tourists ride on one of the park's locomotives.

dren. There is a miniature space needle, a boat ride, and a gigantic playhouse. There is also a theater with shows for children and a petting zoo that includes goats and deer.

Two older locomotives and one new one are used on the Opryland Railroad to take passengers through Opryland. A recording tells passengers about the park. You can get on at two stations. One is in the Western area. The other is in the Hill Country area.

Musical Shows

Opryland USA is not only rides and adventures. It also is a musical show park. That's why it's called "The Home of American Music." While in the park, you may see a band playing. Or you might come across a strolling musician. There can be as many as 12 shows in production at the same time.

Opryland prides itself on the quality of its musical productions. The shows range from country to rock and roll, gospel to Broadway. There are as many as 18 singers and dancers and a 16-piece orchestra in some shows.

The shows are held in several theaters. These include the El Paso Theater and the American Music Theater. There is also the Theater by the Lake and the New Orleans Bandstand. The Country and Bluegrass Theater is a log cabin theater in the Hill Country area.

There also are magical performances for children of all ages in the Kid Stuff Theater. This is next to Big "G" Kid Stuff.

Opryland is open on weekends in the spring and fall and seven days a week in the summer (late May to early September). Some

Opryland's shows range from country to rock and roll, gospel to Broadway.

Performers sing and strum at the Country and Bluegrass Theater.

two and one-half million people now go through the park each year. There is an admission charge that covers all rides and shows for one day. Admission for a second or a third day can be purchased at a reduced price. There is also a fee for parking in the 8,800-space parking lot.

The Grand Ole Opry

Throughout the world, the Grand Ole Opry is identified with country music. It is the longest-running radio show in the world. The first performance of the show was held over 60 years ago. The first performer was an 80-year-old fiddle player named **Uncle Jimmy Thompson.**

The first show took place in an office building in downtown

15

Nashville on November 28, 1925. The show was then called "The WSM Barn Dance" and was broadcast from a fifth floor studio in an insurance company.

It was here that **George D. Hay** introduced Uncle Jimmy. Hay, a young announcer, called himself "The Solemn Old Judge." He gave the program its name in 1927.

Later, the program was moved to a larger studio so that audience reaction could be part of the program. Originally it was mostly an instrumental program. But "singing found its place with the picking" in 1938 when a young Tennessee man, **Roy Acuff,** first took the stage.

Crowds at the show kept growing, and the program kept moving. In 1943, it moved to the 3,000-seat **Ryman Auditorium.** This building was near the Cumberland River in downtown Nashville. Four years earlier, a national network had begun carrying part of the program.

Artists who appeared on the show at the Ryman included many famous names. Among them were Hank Snow, Marty Robbins, Johnny Cash, and Loretta Lynn.

In March 1974, the Grand Ole Opry moved to its present location. This is the 4,400-seat Grand Ole Opry House. This auditorium was to be the centerpiece for Opryland USA.

The Grand Ole Opry House is the world's largest broadcast studio. Its main sound system includes a cluster of 72 speaker horns mounted above the stage. The building is used for events other than the Grand Ole Opry. These include television specials and concerts.

Shows are scheduled every Friday and Saturday night and can be heard on radio station WSM-AM. In the summer tourist months there are up to eight performances of the Opry a week.

Almost a million people come to the Opry every year. They come to hear some of the 60 or so performers on the Opry roster. The stars perform from a 110-foot-wide, 68-foot-deep, maple hardwood-floor stage. Dolly Parton and Barbara Mandrell are among the stars. So are Tom T. Hall, Ricky Skaggs, and Reba McEntire.

Tickets to performances of the Grand Ole Opry are sold in ad-

Roy Clarke and Minnie Pearl perform for a live audience at the Grand Ole Opry.

vance by mail order. All tickets for the Opry are for specific seats. "Reserved" seat tickets are for the main floor and the first balcony. "Upper balcony" tickets are for the second and third balconies. When tickets are still available for a show, they go on sale each Tuesday. The Grand Ole Opry Ticket Office is in the Opryland USA parking lot.

"Music, Music, Music"

Just southeast of the Grand Ole Opry House is the **Acuff Theater.** It seats 1,600 people. Here more than 20 singers and dancers and a 16-piece orchestra put on a musical stage production called "Music, Music, Music." The 75-minute show draws from the musical art of Nashville, Hollywood, and Broadway.

Tickets to this show are sold separately from those for Opryland and the Grand Ole Opry. The show's schedule coincides with Opryland's schedule.

Other Attractions in Opryland USA

Ride a Showboat

While visiting Opryland USA, you'll want to see the *General Jackson*. This giant paddlewheel showboat sails on the Cumberland River.

The four-deck boat is almost 300 feet long and 62 feet wide. It is named after the first steamboat to operate on the river. This

The General Jackson *Showboat and other smaller paddleboats take visitors down the Cumberland River.*

General Jackson boat began operation in 1985.

The boat cruises the Cumberland all year. It sails from its dock just outside the Opryland theme park. There are as many as five cruises a day during the peak summer season.

All cruises offer entertainment. Major musical stage productions are presented in the boat's Victorian Theater, which holds 1,000 people. The shows are produced by the Opryland Entertainment Department. There is an admission charge for the *General Jackson*. Evening cruises include dinner and are more expensive.

Watch the Taping of a TV Show

In Opryland USA, you also can be part of a studio audience and see a television show being taped. The program is a nightly variety show called "Nashville Now."

Opryland has rides for all ages.

Waterfalls, plants, and plenty of sunlight are all part of the Opryland Hotel's lobby.

The program features well-known artists and includes interviews, music, and comedy. Several other shows are also taped there. All tapings are free, but reservations are required for "Nashville Now" and "Crook and Chase." The second show is a weekday magazine series. These two shows are taped every weekday.

Stay at Tennessee's Largest Hotel

The Opryland Hotel is also part of Opryland USA. It is the largest convention hotel property in Tennessee and the 12th largest hotel in the country. It has 1,891 rooms.

The hotel includes two indoor gardens. The Conservatory,

The entrance to the Opryland Hotel is bright, airy, and elegant.

which was completed in 1983, is a garden under glass. A huge skylight connects two wings of guest rooms in the Conservatory. More than 10,000 tropical plants grow in this garden.

The Cascades, completed in 1988, has three waterfalls. The highest is 35 feet. The waterfalls pass over limestone rocks into a 12,500 square foot lake. A fountain lit by laser completes the garden.

Go Sightseeing

Opryland USA also has a sightseeing company. **Grand Ole Opry Sightseeing Tours** offers various tours to sites in the Nashville area. It also offers guided tours to the backstage areas of the Grand Ole Opry House. The tour office is in the Opryland USA parking lot, next to the Grand Ole Opry Ticket Office.

The **Opryland Music Group** has roots in Nashville's oldest music publishing company, Acuff-Rose Publishing. It was founded in 1942 by Roy Acuff and Fred Rose.

Now Opryland Music Group is one of the largest companies in the music industry. It has published a long list of songs. It has made both country and pop hits. Hank Williams and Pee Wee King are two of the writers who have worked here. So have Marty Robbins and the Everly Brothers.

From Music Valley to Downtown Nashville

Music Valley

North of Opryland USA is **Music Valley.** There you will find several different museums. The **Music Valley Wax Museum of the Stars** has over 50 lifelike figures of popular stars. Each is

A huge skylight connects two wings of guest rooms in the Conservatory of the Opryland Hotel.

dressed in a costume donated by a celebrity. It is open daily except for Thanksgiving, Christmas, and New Year's Day. There is an admission charge.

Just to the east of the museum are two more attractions. One is **Cars of the Stars.** It features antique and special-interest cars. The other is **Boxcar Willie's Railroad Museum.** Here you will learn the story of Grand Ole Opry star Boxcar Willie. The museum contains many of Willie's personal possessions as well as railroad artifacts. There is an admission charge for both of these places, and both are open all but three days a year.

Hands-On Museums and Downtown Nashville

Although Nashville is more than 200 years old, it also is a modern city. Millions of dollars have gone into redevelopment. Despite much new construction, however, the city retains the feel of the Old South.

You can begin a tour of downtown Nashville with an educational adventure. Although there is something for the entire family at the Cumberland Science Museum, this museum has kids in mind.

The museum is filled with hands-on exhibits, live animal shows, and health and science programs. You can "travel in space" in the Sudekum Planetarium. You can explore the human body in Health Hall. Younger kids can climb a child-sized spider web in Curiosity Corner. The Hot Air Balloon provides an educational experience in physics. There is an admission charge to the museum, which is closed on Mondays.

Once you are downtown, you might enjoy a walking tour of Nashville. You can begin at the Tennessee State Museum in the heart of downtown. It is located in the James K. Polk Office Building. This building also houses the **Tennessee Performing Arts Center**.

The State Museum offers a look at how people lived many years ago. At the center of the museum is a working gristmill and a reconstructed log cabin. You can see Davy Crockett's rifle and Sam Houston's guitar.

The Tennessee State Museum offers hands-on experiences. There are many programs dealing with different time spans in Tennessee's history. The museum is open daily and admission is free.

If you would like more history, head north a block. Here you will find the **Tennessee State Capitol Building.** This massive

In downtown Nashville, the Tennessee State Capitol Building is brilliantly lit up at night.

JAMES KNOX POLK,
President of the U.S. Born Nov. 2, 1795, Died June 15, 1849.

The mortal remains of
JAMES KNOX POLK,
are resting in the vault beneath.
He was born in Mecklenburg County,
North Carolina,
and emigrated with his father,
Samuel Polk, to Tennessee
in 1806.
The beauty of virtue
was illustrated in his life.
The excellence of Christianity
was exemplified in his death.

SARAH CHILDRESS
WIFE OF JAMES KNOX POLK
1803   1891

building was started in 1845 but wasn't completed until 1859.

James K. Polk is buried here. He was the 11th president of the United States. Statues on the grounds include **Andrew Jackson** and Confederate hero **Sam Davis.** Free tours are offered daily.

Hot or Not, the Crowds Came

Do you remember that the Grand Ole Opry show used to be downtown? Well, head south from the capitol for several blocks. On Fifth Avenue, just north of Broadway, you will find Ryman Auditorium.

Construction of the Ryman was completed in 1892. It was built as a home for religious services. Eventually, it also became the site for major musical performances. Later, it became the city's theater. But its chief claim to fame is that it was the longtime home of the Opry.

At first, the auditorium was not air-conditioned. The temperature inside the building could pass 100 degrees on summer nights. Despite this, people began to line up early on Saturday morning. They wanted to get into that night's Grand Ole Opry performance. By late afternoon, the line was around the building and down Broadway.

The Ryman Auditorium is now a historical landmark. It was listed on the National Register of Historic Places in 1971. There are now guided tours. You can walk across the stage and visit dressing rooms once used by famous country music stars. The building is open to the public daily except Thanksgiving and Christmas. There is an admission charge.

From the Ryman, walk east three blocks to First Avenue North. From here you have a good look at the Cumberland River. You can see Fort Nashborough between Broadway and Church Streets in Riverfront Park.

This fort is a reproduction of the original stockade built by Nashville's first settlers. The present fort includes five reproductions of the original Nashborough cabins. Two are two-story

The gravesite of James K. Polk, the 11th president of the United States, is found on the state capitol grounds.

At Fort Nashborough, tourists can step inside log cabins and see what life was like for pioneers of the 1700s.

blockhouses. They stood at each corner of the fort and were the major defense posts.

The other cabins show different ways of how people lived on the frontier. When the fort was being used, similar cabins housed families. In the present ones, there are fireplaces built of native limestone and wood covered with mud and clay.

The original fort was used until 1792. The reconstruction was built in 1930 and rebuilt in 1962. Fort Nashborough is open Tuesday through Saturday. It is operated by the Metro Nashville Board of Parks and Recreation. A staff in costumes like those worn by the first settlers is on hand during hours of operation. Donations are accepted.

Getting around downtown Nashville is made easier by a shuttle bus service. It operates on weekdays. There is also a shuttle from downtown to Music Row on evenings and weekends.

Music Row

On Music Row, one mile southwest of downtown Nashville, you will find several blocks of museums related to music and performing artists. Many music-related businesses are also located in the area.

If you start on the eastern border of Music Row, you will see three attractions. One is the **Country Music Wax Museum.** Another is the **George Jones Car Collectors Hall of Fame.** The third is the **Hank Williams, Jr., Museum**.

The Country Music Wax Museum is the first wax museum in the world for country music's stars. Over 60 wax figures clothed with original stage costumes are here. Entertainers' instruments and other mementos are also on display.

If you like cars, there are 50 of them in the Car Collectors Hall of Fame. Among them is a 1953 Cadillac owned by George Jones. These is a 1932 Ford rumble seat coupe, powered by Ford's first production V-8 engine. Ford's first production car, a 1903 Model A Ford, is on display, too.

You can also see an Eldorado Cadillac once owned by **Elvis Presley.** The rock star decided after a 1976 concert in Denver, Colorado, that he wanted to buy a car. The car he wanted was in the window of a dealer's showroom. He convinced the dealer to open his store at 2 A.M. He bought that car.

Hank Williams, Sr. and Jr., are the subjects of the Williams Museum. It is one of Nashville's newest attractions. The museum displays Junior's pickup truck. Two videos tell about these country-music legends.

There is an admission fee for all three museums, and all are open daily.

Barbara Mandrell Country

Across Demonbreun Street is **Barbara Mandrell Country.** Here you can get a close look at the family and career of one of country music's best-known stars. It was planned personally by Barbara.

It is filled with mementos, exhibits, and personal items, including costumes, instruments, and other keepsakes from Barbara's stage, television, and movie career. Barbara's bedroom, dressing room, and trophy room are reproduced in exact detail.

You can also see Barbara's luxurious Rolls-Royce, her jewelry collection, and her wedding dress. In addition, you can watch special videos of Barbara's performances and record your personal message to Barbara in "Barbara's autograph book." Barbara Mandrell Country is open daily except New Year's Day. There is an admission charge.

Record Your Own Hit Song

If you want to be a recording star, Music Row will give you that opportunity. You can record a hit song—for a fee. You can do this at the Recording Studios of America, in the same building as Barbara Mandrell Country. The studios are professionally engineered and make twenty-four background tracks available. You can also have a little practice time before your final cut.

A block away is the **Country Music Hall of Fame and Museum**. This museum showcases songwriters, performers, and leaders of the country music industry. Exhibits include those on Johnny Cash, "chart toppers," and the Grand Ole Opry. There are also extensive collections of musical instruments, costumes, records, and films. This museum's hours are subject to change without notice.

The admission fee to the Hall of Fame includes a tour of **RCA's Studio B** on Music Square West. This is where the "Nashville Sound" was born in the 1960s.

Eddy Arnold, Hank Snow, Elvis Presley, and Dolly Parton all recorded their first hits in this studio. Elvis recorded more than 100 songs here. The tour features a demonstration of a recording session.

The lobby floor in the Country Music Hall of Fame and Museum is filled with the names of famous country music stars.

The Country Music Hall of Fame and Museum has exhibits about many of the chart-topping stars of country music.

From City Parks to Music Stars' Homes

A mile further west is **Centennial Park.** The park was the site of the Tennessee Centennial Exposition of 1897. It also is the home of the **Parthenon.** This is the world's only exact-size replica of the ancient Parthenon in Greece. It was completed in 1931, and renovated in 1988.

The Parthenon is accompanied by four art galleries and a 25-foot reproduction of the famous Greek statue of Athena. Greek theater is performed on the building's steps for two weeks in

The Parthenon, an exact replica of the ancient Parthenon in Greece, is found in Nashville's Centennial Park.

mid-summer. The Parthenon is closed Mondays, and there is an admission charge.

South of the park is one of the South's best-known private universities, **Vanderbilt.** Just north of the park are **Meharry College** and **Fisk University.** Fisk's Van Vechten Gallery has an outstanding art collection. The campus of **Tennessee State University** is about a mile north of the park.

In Nashville, you can also take a tour to the homes of country music stars. The popular tour lasts several hours and includes the homes of Dolly Parton, Waylon Jennings, Tammy Wynette, and Johnny Cash. Other tours will take you to the homes of Conway Twitty, Barbara Mandrell, and Roy Acuff. There is a fare for each tour.

From the Hermitage to Hendersonville

Visit the Old South

You can also see two famous 19th-century Southern mansions in Nashville. Visiting them is a lesson in history.

One was the home of Andrew Jackson. He was the seventh president of the United States and the hero of the Battle of New Orleans during the War of 1812. Born in a log cabin, Jackson was nicknamed "Old Hickory" — because he was said to be so tough.

Jackson's home is called the **Hermitage**. It has been called "Tennessee's premier historic attraction." In addition, it has been described as "one of the most beautiful shrines of its kind in the country" and is certified as a national historic landmark.

This beautiful mansion is 12 miles east of downtown, on the north side of Highway 70 North. It is built in the same style as the Tennessee state capitol. The Hermitage looks exactly as it did in the days Jackson lived there.

Jackson moved to Nashville as a young man. He purchased the acreage for the Hermitage in 1804. The site was chosen by his wife, Rachel, who had come to Nashville in the first year of its settlement.

The Jacksons lived in nearby log buildings for 15 years while their mansion was being built. It was completed in 1819. Two wings were added in 1831. Andrew Jackson's wife, Rachel, died in the house in January 1829, shortly before Jackson was inaugurated for the first of his two terms as president.

Unfortunately, most of the mansion was destroyed by fire in 1834. Jackson was then in Washington, D.C., serving his second term as president. The president decided to reconstruct his home; the reconstructed mansion is what you see today.

The mansion is on 625 acres of gentle, rolling farmland. There

The Hermitage is a beautiful mansion and was the home of Andrew Jackson, the seventh president of the United States.

are large cedars, maples, and poplars at the Hermitage. The hickory trees on the grounds were planted more than 150 years ago.

On the property are the mansion, two log houses, a carriage house, and a formal garden. The garden was designed for Rachel in 1819 and is maintained with the same flowers and herbs that she grew. The garden is also the burial place of Rachel and Andrew Jackson and members of their family.

The mansion is furnished with original family pieces. These include furniture, silver, glassware, and paintings. Some of the artifacts at the Hermitage are related to Jackson's military career and his years as president.

The Hermitage is open daily except Thanksgiving and Christmas. There is an admission charge.

Across the street from the Hermitage is **Tulip Grove**. This was the home of Andrew Jackson Donelson, Rachel's nephew. Donelson served as Jackson's secretary while he was president. The admission charge to The Hermitage includes a visit to Tulip Grove.

"Queen of the Tennessee Plantations"

Another Southern showplace is **Belle Meade Mansion.** It was once the mansion house of a 5,300-acre plantation. The name means beautiful meadow. It was the home of **John Harding** and his family and the showplace of middle Tennessee from 1853 to 1904. The Confederate Army used it as a headquarters during the Battle of Nashville.

The Harding family also made Belle Meade a famous horse farm. It was one of the first thoroughbred horse-breeding farms in the country. By 1902 it was known as the "oldest and greatest" American thoroughbred nursery. Horsemen came there each year for the annual auction of yearling colts.

The last horses were sold in 1902. Two years later the property itself was auctioned. Today 24 acres remain. This land, the mansion, and eight outbuildings belong to a nonprofit organization created to preserve historic sites.

The mansion was recently renovated. Inside are furnishings showing the life of a bygone time and oil paintings of famous horses. At the rear of the mansion is a large carriage house and stable. Here you can see one of the South's best collections of carriages.

Belle Meade is seven miles southwest of downtown Nashville. It is open daily, and there is an admission charge.

Not far west of Belle Meade is another historical restoration. **Travellers' Rest** is where Andrew Jackson held several political strategy meetings. Travellers' Rest was built in 1799 by John Overton, Jackson's law partner and presidential campaign manager.

From 1853 to 1904, the Belle Meade Mansion was the showplace of Tennessee.

Visitors today can see a functioning weaving house, a smokehouse, and a formal garden. It is open daily, and there is an entrance fee.

Cash, Twitty, and Can after Can

For a further look at modern life, you can make the trip to **Hendersonville, Tennessee,** about 20 miles northeast of downtown Nashville. That's the location of the **House of Cash** and **Twitty City/Music Village USA.**

The House of Cash is a showcase for many of the personal possessions of Johnny Cash and June Carter. There is an admission charge. It is closed on Sundays and from November 1 through March 14.

Country music star Conway Twitty sits in front of the 15-acre Twitty City/Music Village USA.

Twitty City/Music Village USA is the home of country superstar Conway Twitty and his children. It is also a 15-acre tourist complex that offers regular live entertainment. Thanksgiving weekend through the first weekend of January is "Christmas at Twitty City." Featured are over 50 displays and 350,000 lights.

Music Village USA is a complex containing museums of Ferlin Husky, Bill Monroe, and Marty Robbins—three country music stars. There are admission charges to Twitty City/Music Village USA; it is open throughout the year.

Head a few miles west of Hendersonville to **Goodlettsville**, where you can see the country's largest collection of antique beer and soda cans. More than 25,000 cans are on display at the **Museum of Beverage Containers & Advertising**, along with thousands of period advertising pieces. The museum, on Ridgecrest Drive, is open daily, and there is an admission charge.

If you're in Nashville around December 1, you can see the mansion of country music performer Tom T. Hall. This is at Fox Hollow near **Franklin, Tennessee.** It is about 20 miles south of downtown.

Memphis and Graceland

Nashville is where the late rock superstar Elvis Presley lived. But it is in Memphis, a city southwest of Nashville, where **Graceland,** Presley's former home, can be found.

Memphis is about 210 miles from Nashville on Interstate 40. It is on the Mississippi River in the southwest corner of Tennessee. Some 650,000 people live there. The city is a busy river port and is also a leading medical center.

Once in town, you can follow the "Tour Memphis" directional street signs. They will take you to the Visitors' Information Center on Beale Street.

Graceland was where "the king of rock and roll" lived. It is about 10 miles south of downtown Memphis. If you visit Graceland, you will be among thousands who flock here each year. People come to experience the private world of Elvis Presley. The crowds are even larger each August 16. They come to observe the anniversary of Elvis Presley's death on August 16, 1977.

Visits begin at Graceland Plaza, across the street from the mansion. During the tour, you will see the music room and its 24-carat gold concert grand piano. This guided tour also includes Elvis's trophy building, where his stage costumes and his collection of gold records and other awards are displayed. Also included in this tour are the mansion grounds. Elvis is buried in Meditation Gardens.

Another tour takes you aboard the *Lisa Marie* jet. This is the plane Elvis named for his daughter.

A third tour takes you through the "Elvis—Up Close" mini-museum. This tour is "an intimate look at the private side of Elvis." Visitors can also check out Elvis's collection of vehicles, including his famous pink 1955 Cadillac.

There is an admission charge for each tour. Tickets can be purchased at Graceland Plaza. Graceland is open daily March through October, but is closed on Tuesdays from November through February. It also is closed on Thanksgiving, Christmas, and New Year's Day.

You don't have to be a country music lover to enjoy Nashville, but you might become one during your visit.

Brush up on your country music and head south. Nashville is a city rooted in our country's past, yet it is a modern city because of its businesses and music.

Nashville offers you a unique theme park in Opryland. You can also soak up the sights and sounds of America's music. If you're a country music fan it will be a visit you'll always remember. And if you aren't, you could become one before you head home.

Head south to Nashville, Tennessee — Music City, U.S.A.

Nashville Statistics

Nashville: Named after General Francis Nash. The city's original name was Nashborough.

1819: The year steamboats began operating on the Cumberland River

1854: The year railroads came to Nashville

Number of churches: 700

Number of convention halls and auditoriums: 7

Herschel Greer Stadium: Home of the Nashville Sounds, professional basketball team

Opryland: Open seven days a week in the summer and on weekends in the spring and fall

Opryland Hotel: Currently has 1,891 rooms. The hotel opened in 1977 with only 600 rooms.

The Nashville Network: Runs six hours of new programming a day and is on the air 18 hours a day.

For More Information

For more information about Nashville, write to:

Department of Tourism
320 Sixth Avenue N.
Rachel Jackson Building, 5th floor
Nashville, TN 37219

For information about Opryland USA, write to:

Opryland USA Customer Service
2802 Opryland Drive
Nashville, TN 37214

For schedules of TV show tapings, write to:

TNN Viewer Services
2806 Opryland Drive
Nashville, TN 37214

City Map

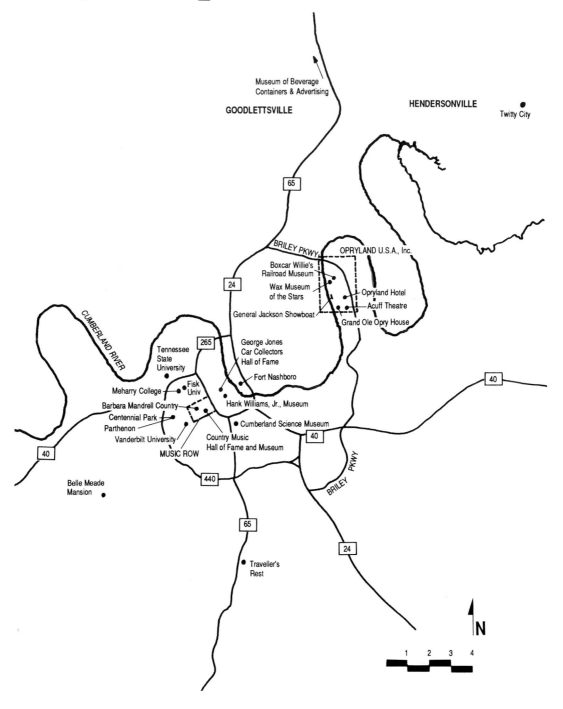

Museum of Beverage
Containers & Advertising

GOODLETTSVILLE

HENDERSONVILLE

Twitty City

65

BRILEY PKWY

OPRYLAND U.S.A., Inc.

24

Boxcar Willie's
Railroad Museum

Wax Museum
of the Stars

Opryland Hotel

Acuff Theatre

General Jackson Showboat

Grand Ole Opry House

CUMBERLAND RIVER

265

George Jones
Car Collectors
Hall of Fame

Tennessee
State
University

Fort Nashboro

40

Meharry College

Fisk
Univ

Barbara Mandrell Country

Hank Williams, Jr., Museum

Centennial Park

Cumberland Science Museum

Parthenon

Vanderbilt University

Country Music
Hall of Fame and Museum

40

BRILEY PKWY

MUSIC ROW

40

440

Belle Meade
Mansion

65

24

Traveller's
Rest

N

1   2   3   4

Nashville, Tennessee

Index
of People & Places